IRELAND
Geography Activity Book for Kids

Perfect for Young Explorers!

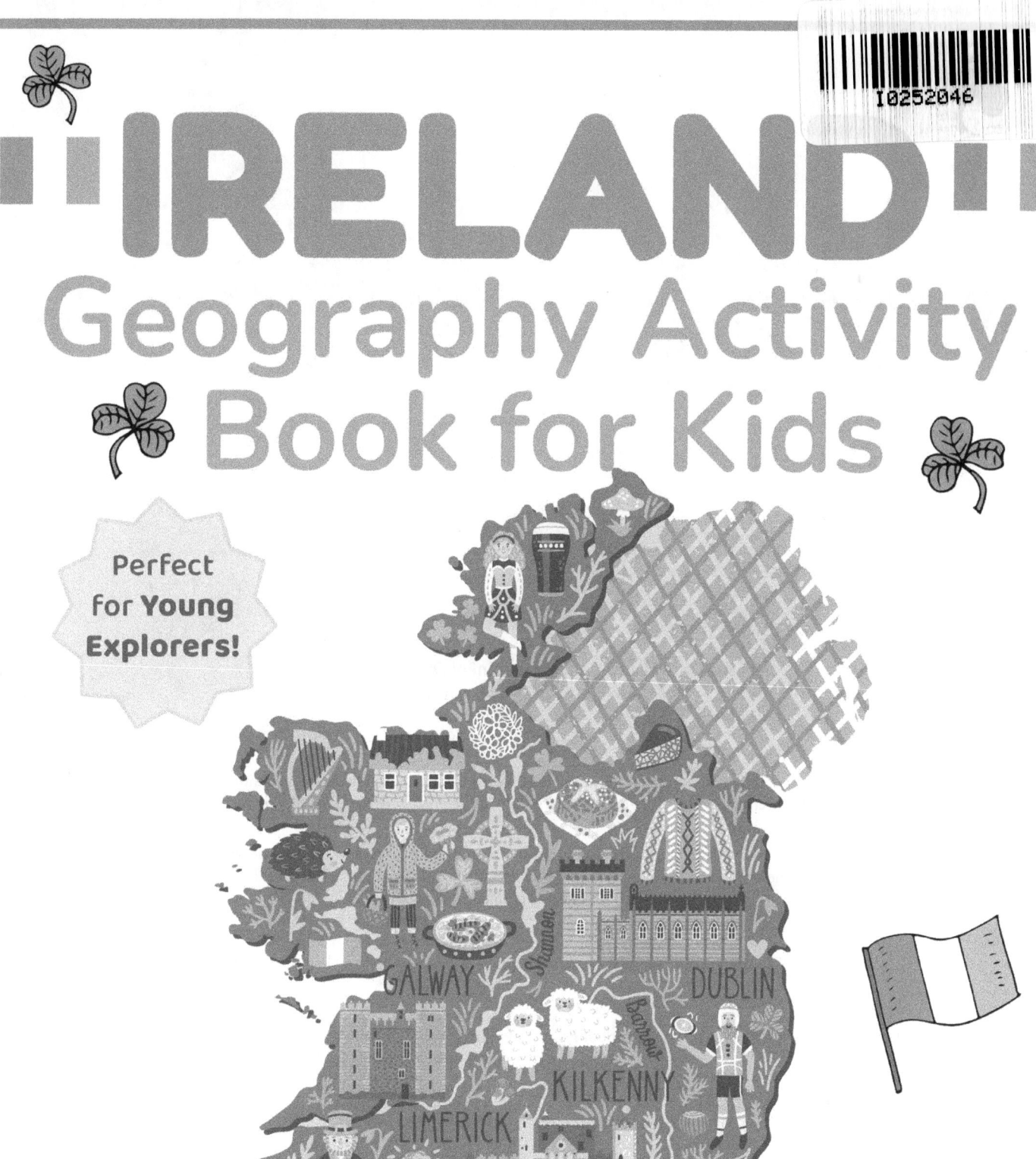

Fun Facts, Puzzles, Maps, Legends, and More
Learn About Irish Culture, History, and Landmarks

Published by Dylanna Press an imprint of Dylanna Publishing, Inc.
Copyright © 2025 by Dylanna Press

Editor: Julie Grady

All rights reserved. No part of this publication may be reproduced, stored in a retrieval system, or transmitted by any means, including electronic, mechanical, photocopying, or otherwise, without prior written permission of the publisher.

Limit of liability/Disclaimer of Warranty: The Publisher and the author make no representations or warranties with respect to the accuracy or completeness of the contents of this work and specifically disclaim all warranties, including without limitation warranties of fitness for a particular purpose.

Although the publisher has taken all reasonable care in the preparation of this book, we make no warranty about the accuracy or completeness of its content and, to the maximum extent permitted, disclaim all liability arising from its use.

Trademarks: Dylanna Press is a registered trademark of Dylanna Publishing, Inc. and may not be used without written permission.
info@dylannapubishing.com

WELCOME TO IRELAND!

Get ready for an exciting journey through one of the most magical places in the world—Ireland, also known as the Emerald Isle! This book is packed with fun facts, cool activities, and amazing discoveries that will help you learn all about a country filled with green hills, ancient legends, friendly people, and incredible places.

Ireland is a land of castles, cliffs, music, myths, and more. You'll explore stone forts and mysterious tombs, meet heroes and poets, and even learn how to say a few words in Irish Gaelic!

Some parts of Ireland feel like they come from fairy tales—there are ancient forests, hidden lakes, foggy mountains, and even stories of leprechauns guarding pots of gold at the ends of rainbows. Other parts are full of life and energy, like the buzzing streets of Dublin, where you'll find live music, cheerful shops, and beautiful old buildings.

In this book, you'll:

- Explore famous cities, natural wonders, and fascinating landmarks
- Learn about ancient Celts, St. Patrick, and Irish independence
- Discover traditional music, dancing, holidays, and delicious food
- Play games, solve puzzles, color pictures, and read legends!

Whether you're visiting Ireland, learning from home, or just curious about this amazing country, you're about to uncover what makes Ireland unique, proud, and full of personality.

So grab your pencil—and maybe a shamrock cookie or two—and let's start our adventure!

Quick Facts about Ireland

- **Official Name:** Republic of Ireland (Éire)
- **Capital:** Dublin
- **Nickname:** Emerald Isle
- **Population:** About 5 million
- **Currency:** Euro (€)
- **Languages:** English and Irish (Gaeilge)
- **Government:** Parliamentary democracy

MAP OF IRELAND

Before we dive into Ireland's amazing places, let's get to know where everything is! Ireland is an island located in northwestern Europe. It's surrounded by the Atlantic Ocean and shares its northeastern border with Northern Ireland, which is part of the United Kingdom.

Ireland is divided into four provinces and 32 counties. The four provinces are:

- Leinster (East – includes Dublin, the capital)
- Munster (South – home to Cork and Limerick)
- Connacht (West – full of wild beauty and Atlantic coastlines)
- Ulster (North – only part of this province is in the Republic)

You'll also find rivers, lakes, mountains, and a long, rugged coastline filled with beaches, cliffs, and fishing villages.

Color the Flag

The flag of Ireland is called the tricolor (say: TRY-color) because it has three vertical stripes. Each color has a special meaning:
- Green stands for Irish Catholics and the country's Gaelic traditions.
- Orange represents Irish Protestants and the followers of William of Orange.
- White is the color of peace and unity between the two sides.

The flag was first flown in 1848 as a symbol of hope for a united Ireland. It officially became the national flag when Ireland gained independence in the 1900s.

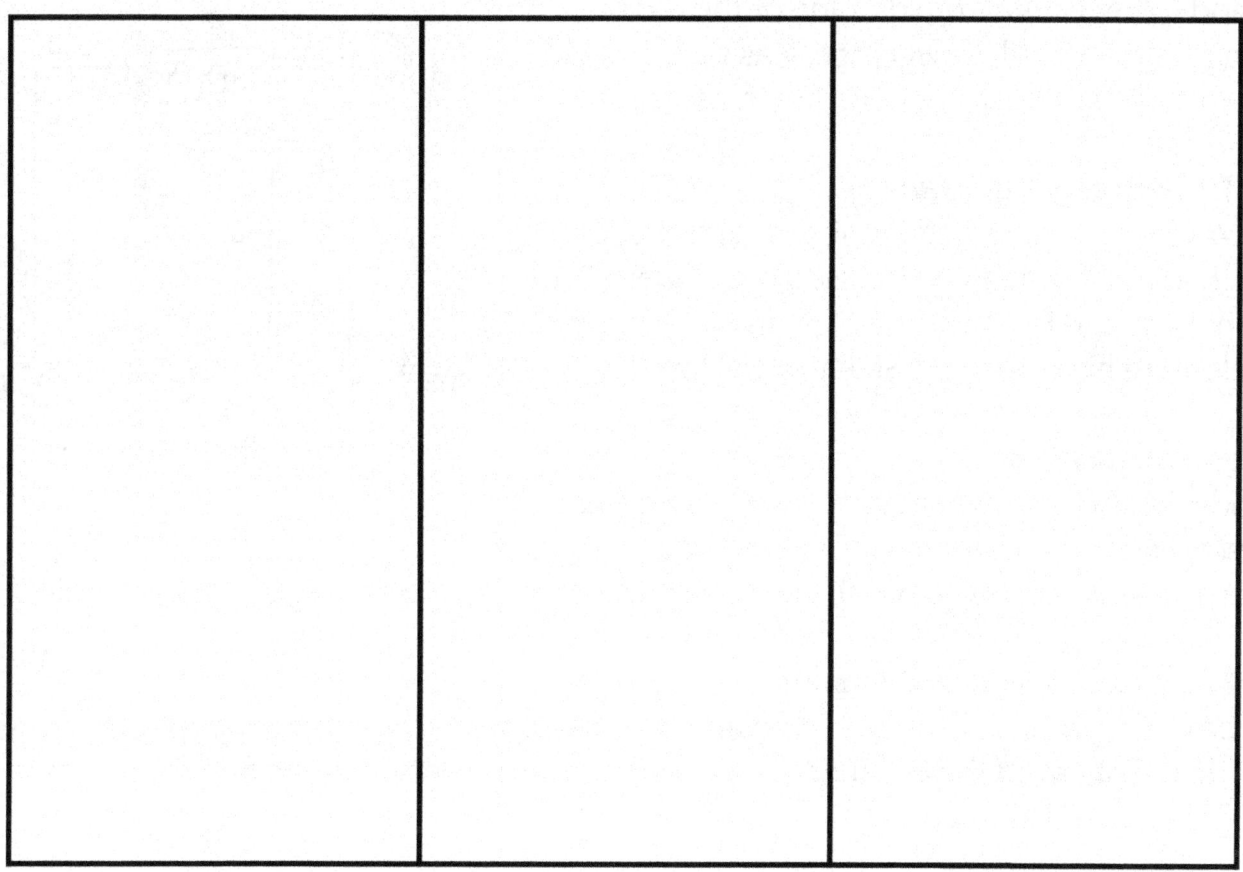

Color Guide: Left stripe = Green; Middle stripe = White; Right stripe = Orange

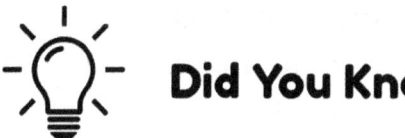 **Did You Know?**

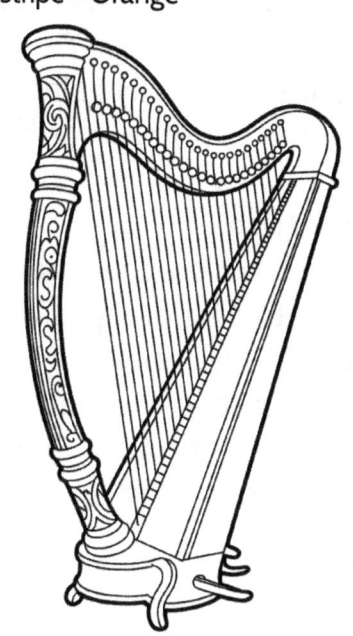

- The harp, not the shamrock, is Ireland's official national symbol.
- Ireland is called the Emerald Isle because it's so green.
- Over 70 million people around the world have Irish roots!
- Irish (Gaeilge) is one of Europe's oldest languages.

A Short History of Ireland

Ireland's history stretches back thousands of years—filled with ancient monuments, brave heroes, and a long fight for freedom.

Ancient Times
The first people arrived in Ireland over 9,000 years ago. Later came the Celts, who brought their own language, music, and myths. They built forts and followed wise druids. One of the oldest buildings in the world, Newgrange, was built around 3200 BCE—even older than the pyramids!

Saint Patrick and Christianity
In the 400s, a man named Patrick came to Ireland to teach about Christianity. He used the shamrock to explain ideas and became a saint. Many Irish people still celebrate him today on St. Patrick's Day.

Vikings and Castles
Around 800 AD, Vikings sailed to Ireland and started towns like Dublin. Later, Normans arrived from France and built castles across the land. Irish clans ruled different regions for centuries.

British Rule and the Great Famine
Over time, England took control of Ireland. Life became hard for many people. In the 1840s, a terrible event called the Great Famine happened when potato crops failed. Millions of people died or moved away.

The Fight for Independence
In the early 1900s, Irish people began fighting for freedom. After events like the Easter Rising of 1916, Ireland finally gained independence from Britain in 1922. But not all of Ireland became a new country—Northern Ireland stayed part of the United Kingdom.

Modern Times
Today, Ireland is a peaceful, democratic country known for its rich culture, beautiful landscapes, and strong communities. It joined the European Union in 1973, and cities like Dublin are now home to writers, artists, and tech companies. Peace agreements like the Good Friday Agreement (1998) helped bring stability between Ireland and Northern Ireland, and Irish traditions continue to thrive around the world.

Timeline of Major Events

- **3200 BCE** — Newgrange is built—older than the pyramids!
- **500s BCE** — Celtic tribes arrive in Ireland.
- **432 CE** — St. Patrick begins spreading Christianity.
- **800s** — Vikings raid and settle in Ireland.
- **1169** — Norman invaders from England arrive.
- **1541** — King Henry VIII declares himself King of Ireland.
- **1845–1849** — Great Famine causes 1 million deaths and mass emigration.
- **1916** — Easter Rising—a major rebellion for Irish independence.
- **1922** — Most of Ireland becomes independent as the Irish Free State.
- **1949** — Ireland officially becomes the Republic of Ireland.
- **1973** — Ireland joins the European Union.
- **1998** — The Good Friday Agreement brings peace in Northern Ireland.

Newgrange: Older Than the Pyramids!

Deep in the green hills of County Meath sits one of the most amazing ancient buildings in the world: Newgrange. It's a giant stone tomb built over 5,000 years ago.

Newgrange was made by early farmers using giant stones stacked into a dome. It has a long passage that leads to a secret chamber inside. Nobody knows for sure what it was used for—maybe for burials, or for ceremonies honoring the sun and stars.

Here's the coolest part: once a year, at sunrise on the winter solstice (the shortest day of the year), a beam of sunlight shines perfectly through the passage and lights up the inside chamber. That means the people who built it understood the sun and seasons very well!

You can still visit Newgrange today and see the white stone walls, carved spirals, and grassy roof—it looks like a magical hill straight out of a legend.

Cities and Landmarks Word Search

```
L I M E R I C K Q D R T N S Y
X V M A S R J F A C E B Y H B
M V M R Z C M T V J H S P A J
A E G N A R G W E N O O B N B
H R W D X W Q K Y S M Q K N O
G Y A K U U D E S Y F Q H O Y
A N P N W B N A A K O O I N N
O N W A I R L W R E S G X E E
R E K I A S E I L Q F A U L R
C K K L C S L G N G F L Q Z I
M L L E U K N A J Z I W O M V
T I H A R I L I N K L A C K E
K K C G D R O O N D C Y L R R
L V Z O T H Y V W Q S S Q O I
U G L E N D A L O U G H P C B
R D O N E G A L W N E R R U B
F R C L U Y N X H V E R A L C
V G W Z L Y G I L L E K S B I
```

Aran Islands   Croagh   Kilkenny
Boyne River   Dingle   Killarney
Burren   Donegal   Limerick
Causeway   Dublin   Newgrange
Clare   Galway   Shannon
Cliffs Of Moher Glendalough Skellig
Cork   Kerry   Wicklow

Government

Ireland is a parliamentary democracy. That means the people vote to choose their leaders, and the government makes the laws.

Ireland's laws are made by a group called the Oireachtas, which is the national parliament. It meets in Dublin and has two parts: the Dáil Éireann and the Seanad Éireann. Members of the Dáil are elected by the people to speak for them and make decisions.

The leader of the government is called the Taoiseach (say: TEE-shock), which is the Irish word for Prime Minister. The Taoiseach is chosen from the elected members of the Dáil and works with other officials to run the country.

Ireland also has a President, who is the head of state. The president represents the country at official events, but doesn't make the laws or run the government.

Everyone in Ireland must follow the law, and adults can vote in elections to help choose the country's leaders.

This is where the Irish Parliament meets—it's called Leinster House and it's located in Dublin.

National Symbols

NATIONAL TREE

Sessile Oak

NATIONAL PLANT

Shamrock

NATIONAL ANIMAL

Irish Hare

NATIONAL BIRD

Northern Lapwing

County Map

Ireland's Provinces and Counties

Ireland is made up of **26 counties**, and those counties are grouped into **four provinces**. Each province has its own traditions, accents, and local pride—especially when it comes to sports! Take a look at the map on the previous page. Can you find which counties belong to each province?

....

The Four Provinces

Leinster
This is the eastern province. It's home to Ireland's capital city and many busy towns and farmlands.
Counties in Leinster:
Dublin, Wicklow, Kildare, Meath, Louth, Laois, Offaly, Westmeath, Longford, Carlow, Kilkenny, Wexford

Munster
Located in the south and southwest, Munster is famous for its coastline, castles, and rugged mountains.
Counties in Munster:
Cork, Kerry, Limerick, Clare, Tipperary, Waterford

Connacht
This western province is known for wild scenery, Irish-speaking areas, and strong traditions in music and sport.
Counties in Connacht:
Galway, Mayo, Sligo, Roscommon, Leitrim

Ulster
Most of Ulster is part of Northern Ireland, but three counties are in the Republic.
Counties in Ulster:
Donegal, Monaghan, Cavan

....

Try This!

- **Color the counties** in your favorite province all the same shade.
- **Draw a border** around each province group on the map.
- **Pick a county** and look it up—what's it famous for?

Saint Patrick: Ireland's Patron Saint

Over 1,500 years ago, a boy named Patrick was captured by pirates and taken from Britain to Ireland. He was made to work as a shepherd, watching sheep alone in the hills. After several years, he escaped and returned home—but he never forgot Ireland.

Later in life, Patrick became a Christian missionary. He felt called to go back to Ireland—not as a prisoner, but to teach and help people. He traveled across the island, sharing his beliefs and building churches.

Patrick is most famous for using a shamrock to explain a religious idea: how something could be three parts in one whole—just like the shamrock has three leaves. That's why shamrocks are still a symbol of Ireland today.

There's also a legend that Saint Patrick drove all the snakes out of Ireland by chasing them into the sea. While there probably weren't any snakes there to begin with, it's a fun story that adds to his legend!

Discover Ireland Crossword

Use what you've learned in this book to solve the puzzle.

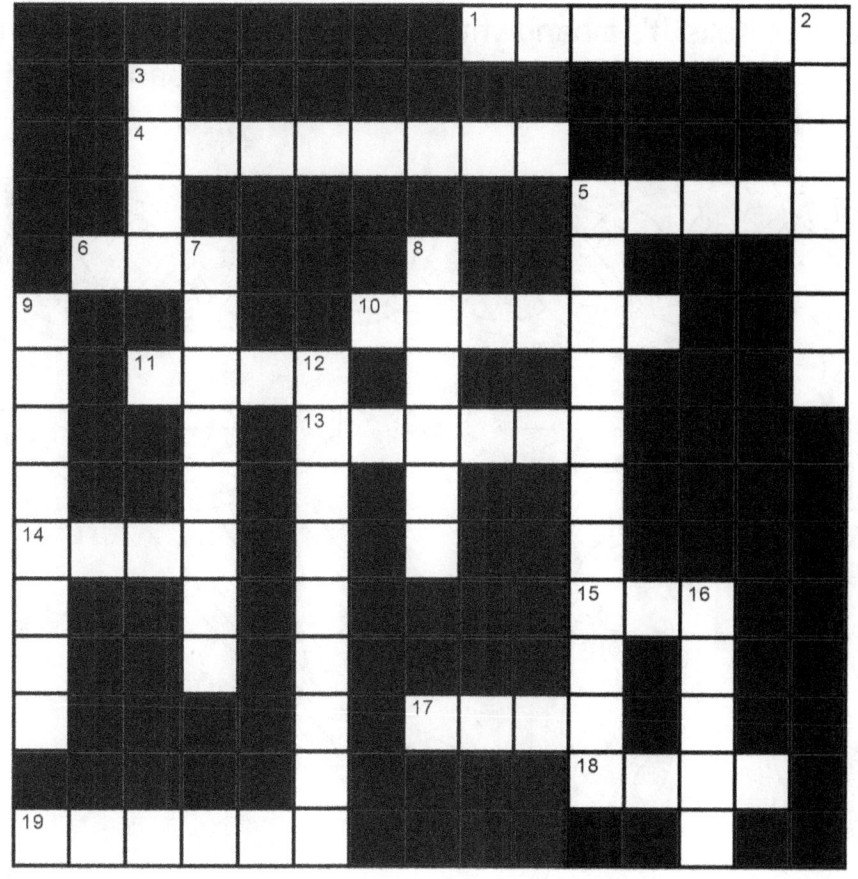

Across

1 Many of these old buildings are in ruins now (7)
4 Ocean to the west of Ireland (8)
5 Color associated with Ireland (5)
6 Helps you find where places are (3)
10 Rocky landscape in County Clare (6)
11 County that's home to Blarney Castle (4)
13 Ireland is one! (6)
14 This falls from the sky a lot in Ireland (4)
15 Most common trees in Irish forests (3)
17 It's green, white, and orange (4)
18 Instrument that is national symbol (4)
19 Ireland is divided into 26 of these (6)

Down

2 Longest river in Ireland (7)
3 Hill where the ancient High Kings rules (4)
5 Monastic site with round towers (11)
7 There are 4 of these big regions in Ireland (8)
8 Capital city (6)
9 Ireland's lucky green plant (8)
12 National park with lakes and red deer (9)
16 County famous for the Ring of _____ (5)

Book of Kells

Over 1,200 years ago, Irish monks created one of the most beautiful books in the world: the Book of Kells. It's a handwritten copy of the four Christian gospels—but it's also filled with bright colors, golden details, and incredible designs.

The book was made on vellum (a type of animal skin) using quill pens and natural inks. It has hundreds of decorated pages, with swirling Celtic knots, mythical animals, and large letters turned into works of art.

No one knows exactly where it was created, but many believe it started on the island of Iona, off the coast of Scotland, and was later brought to Kells in Ireland for safety.

Today, the Book of Kells is kept at Trinity College in Dublin, where people from all over the world come to see it. Even after more than a thousand years, the pages still look amazing!

Landmark Matching Game

Match the landmarks with their descriptions.

 **Cliffs of Moher** | An island with an ancient monastery and steep stone steps

 **Newgrange** | Huge cliffs towering over the Atlantic Ocean in County Clare

 **Blarney Castle** | A stone tomb older than the pyramids, built by ancient people

 **Rock of Cashel** | A hilltop ruin once home to Irish kings and church leaders

 **Skellig Michael** | A quiet valley with a round tower and old monastic buildings

 **Glendalough** | A medieval castle where people kiss a stone for good luck

Famous People from Ireland

Ireland has been home to many world-changing thinkers, artists, scientists, and leaders. Meet some of the most famous!

Robert Boyle

Robert Boyle was a brilliant scientist who changed the way people studied the world. He was born in Lismore, County Waterford, in 1627. At a time when science and magic were often mixed up, Boyle believed in testing ideas with experiments—something we still do in science today.

He is most famous for Boyle's Law, which explains how gas pressure and volume are connected. This discovery helped shape modern chemistry and physics. He also studied air, sound, fire, and even created one of the first air pumps!

Boyle was curious about everything and believed science should be used to help people. Even though he lived hundreds of years ago, his ideas are still part of science classrooms today.

Daniel O'Connell

Daniel O'Connell was one of Ireland's most important political leaders. Born in County Kerry in 1775, he became a powerful voice for Catholic rights at a time when many Irish people were not allowed to vote or hold public office.

O'Connell believed in peaceful protest instead of violence. He gave powerful speeches, led massive rallies called "monster meetings," and helped pass a law that allowed Catholics to serve in Parliament. Because of this, people called him "The Liberator." Today, O'Connell is remembered as a hero who used words—not weapons—to change his country for the better.

Bram Stoker

Bram Stoker is best known as the author of Dracula, one of the most famous horror stories ever written. He was born in Dublin in 1847 and loved reading spooky tales and heroic legends as a child.

Before becoming a writer, Stoker worked as a theater manager and wrote books in his free time. In 1897, he published Dracula—a chilling story about a mysterious vampire from Transylvania. The book became a worldwide hit and helped shape how people imagine vampires even today.

Stoker's writing mixed Irish storytelling traditions with gothic mystery. While Dracula is his most famous book, he also wrote other adventure and ghost stories filled with suspense and strange happenings.

W. B. Yeats

William Butler Yeats is one of Ireland's most famous writers. He loved Irish legends, magical stories, and the wild landscapes of the west. His poems often mixed myth and mystery with big questions about life, love, and change.

Yeats helped start the Irish Literary Revival—a movement to celebrate Irish culture and language through books and plays. He also helped found the Abbey Theatre in Dublin, which became Ireland's national theater.

In 1923, Yeats became the first Irish person to win the Nobel Prize for Literature. He believed in the power of words to shape a nation, and many of his poems are still studied and loved around the world today.

Mary Robinson

Mary Robinson made history in 1990 when she became the first woman to be elected President of Ireland. Before that, she was a lawyer, teacher, and a strong voice for people who didn't always have one—especially women, refugees, and those facing poverty.

As president, she was known for being kind, fair, and willing to speak up. She helped modernize Ireland's image and opened the doors of the presidential home to the public for the first time. People admired her for listening to ordinary citizens, not just politicians.

After her time as president, she continued her work around the world. She became the United Nations High Commissioner for Human Rights, traveling to many countries to help protect people's freedoms and basic rights.

Enya

Enya is one of the most famous singers ever to come from Ireland. Born Eithne Ní Bhraonáin in County Donegal, she grew up speaking Irish and surrounded by music. Her family was part of a traditional band, but Enya found her own style—calm, dreamy, and unlike anything else.

She became famous around the world for songs like "Orinoco Flow" and "Only Time." Her music often features layered vocals, gentle piano, and Celtic melodies, and she sometimes sings in Irish as well as English and Latin.

Enya is known for being very private, but her music has reached millions of fans in dozens of countries. She has sold over 80 million albums and brought a peaceful, magical Irish sound to the world stage.

Maze Game

Help the leprechaun find the pot of gold.

St. Patrick's Day Celebration

St. Patrick's Day is celebrated every March 17th, and it's a big deal in Ireland! People wear green, paint shamrocks on their faces, and enjoy lively parades filled with music, costumes, and Irish dancing.

The holiday honors St. Patrick, who brought Christianity to Ireland. But it's also a joyful celebration of Irish culture, with traditional food, crafts, and storytelling. Whether you're marching in a parade or eating green cupcakes, it's a day to feel proud and festive.

Bonfire Night (St. John's Eve)

On the night of June 23, people in parts of Ireland celebrate Bonfire Night, also known as St. John's Eve. Families and neighbors gather to build big bonfires in open fields or by the sea. As the sun sets, flames light up the sky—and the celebration begins!

This tradition goes back to ancient Celtic times, when midsummer was seen as a magical turning point in the year. Lighting fires was believed to protect crops, animals, and people from harm. Later, the Christian holiday of St. John's Day blended with these older beliefs, and the bonfire tradition continued.

Today, people still mark the night with music, stories, dancing, and sometimes food cooked over the fire. It's a way to celebrate summer and remember Ireland's long history of seasonal festivals.

Traditions and Holidays Word Search

```
K K I L X K C O R M A H S F H
L N D P O T I G N I C N A D I
M Y R V P R A H I F R R A V G
B H U R L I N G K W V N L E S
O K P A W D O J T Q U Y R N I
D Q G S C W G R B A C I V F L
H K M R T A E R H D F E K W I
R H E K A V M C E N L P C A E
A A I T O I E O O E J K I U C
N N N L J R N B G E N C R C F
Z D C X P K B B T I L M T I N
E F K E Q D N N O K E U A L R
D A L B W T O M E W K S P E H
A S F O Y V P X G P A I T A E
R T E S O L S T I C E C S G X
A I A F I D D L E O B N D H I
P N S O R L U P G E V A I E Q
U G T X Y A D Y A M V I V R J
```

Bodhran
Bonfire
Camogie
Ceili
Clover
Dancing
Feast

Fiddle
Gaelic
Green
Handfasting
Harp
Hurling
Leprechaun

May Day
Music
Parade
Rainbow
Shamrock
Solstice
St Patrick

Irish Dancing

Irish dancing is fast, fun, and full of rhythm! Dancers keep their upper bodies still while their feet move quickly in patterns. It's usually performed in colorful dresses and hard shoes that tap on the floor like drums.

Irish dancing is seen at festivals, St. Patrick's Day celebrations, and competitions called feise-anna (pronounced "fesh-uh-nuh"). The energy and precision of the dancers are so exciting, you might just want to jump up and try it yourself!

May Day (Bealtaine) — Welcoming Summer in Ireland

In old Ireland, the beginning of May was a time to welcome the summer and celebrate nature's return to life. This holiday is called Bealtaine (pronounced BYOWL-tin-uh) and was one of the four big festivals of the ancient Celtic calendar.

Long ago, people lit bonfires to protect their homes and animals from harm and to mark the changing season. Some led their cattle between two fires for luck, and others hung rowan branches or flowers above their doorways to keep away bad spirits.

Today, some people still celebrate May Day by decorating bushes or trees with ribbons, eggshells, and flowers—a tradition called the May Bush. It's a fun way to honor Irish history and the arrival of longer, warmer days.

Decorate your own May Bush!
Draw a little tree and add colorful paper ribbons, flowers, and lucky charms.

Samhain – The Celtic Origins of Halloween

Long before Halloween existed, people in ancient Ireland celebrated Samhain (pronounced SOW-in). It marked the end of the harvest and the beginning of the dark half of the year—right around October 31.

The Celts believed that on this night, the barrier between the living and spirit worlds grew thin. People lit bonfires to keep away evil spirits, wore costumes and masks to hide from wandering ghosts, and left out food offerings for friendly visitors from the other side.

> **Did You Know?**
>
> Instead of pumpkins, people in Ireland used to carve turnips into spooky lanterns!

Many of today's Halloween traditions—like dressing up, carving pumpkins, and trick-or-treating—have their roots in Samhain. It was a time of both celebration and caution, as people welcomed the new season and remembered those who had passed.

The Children of Lir

LONG AGO, WHEN magic flowed through Ireland like morning mist through the valleys, there lived a great sea god named Lir. His palace beneath the waves was filled with treasures beyond counting, but his greatest treasures were his four beloved children: Aodh, Fionnuala, Fiachra, and Conn.

Aodh was the eldest, brave and strong like his father. Fionnuala was the only daughter, with hair like spun gold and a voice so beautiful that even the birds stopped singing to listen. Fiachra and Conn were the youngest, twin boys who were never far from each other's side.

The children lived happily in their father's palace until the day Lir decided to take a new wife. Her name was Aoife, and she was beautiful and graceful, but her heart harbored a terrible jealousy.

At first, Aoife tried to love the children, but every day she watched as Lir showered them with affection. Every evening, she listened as he told them stories and sang them to sleep. Every morning, she saw how his eyes lit up when they ran to greet him.

"He loves them more than me," Aoife whispered to herself in the darkness of their chamber. "They have taken my place in his heart."

This jealousy grew like a poisonous vine until it consumed all the good in Aoife's heart. She began to plot against the innocent children, planning a revenge so cruel that even the sea itself would weep.

One bright summer morning, Aoife called to the children. "Come, my dears," she said with a false smile. "Let us go to the lake for a swim. The water is perfect today."

The children, trusting and innocent, eagerly agreed. Fionnuala picked wildflowers as they walked, while the three boys chased butterflies through the meadows. They had no idea that this would be their last day as human children.

When they reached the shore of Lough Derravaragh, the children splashed joyfully in the crystal-clear water. Aoife watched them play, and for a moment, her heart softened. They looked so happy, so full of life and laughter.

But jealousy is a powerful poison, and it quickly hardened her heart again. Raising her arms to the sky, Aoife began to chant in the ancient language of magic.

"By the power of darkness, by the strength of my will, let these children be changed, let my curse be fulfilled!"

A terrible wind began to blow, and the sky darkened with unnatural clouds. The children felt a strange tingling in their arms and legs, and they cried out in fear as white feathers began to sprout from their skin.

"Aoife!" Fionnuala gasped as her golden hair transformed into gleaming white plumage. "What are you doing to us?"

"I am taking my revenge," Aoife replied coldly. "You have stolen my husband's love, so now you shall be swans upon the lake. But because I am not completely heartless, I grant you one mercy – you shall keep your human voices and the gift of beautiful song."

The transformation was complete. Where four children had stood, four magnificent swans now floated on the dark water. Their feathers were pure white as fresh snow, their necks graceful as dancer's arms, but their eyes held all the intelligence and sadness of their human souls.

"Please," Fionnuala begged, her voice now hauntingly beautiful as it echoed across the water. "Change us back. We have done nothing to deserve this fate."

But Aoife's heart was stone. "The spell cannot be broken until you hear the sound of Christian bells ringing across the land, and even then, only after you have spent three hundred years on Lough Derravaragh, three hundred years on the sea between

Ireland and Scotland, and three hundred years near the Isle of Inishglora. Nine hundred years you shall remain as swans."

With that cruel pronouncement, Aoife disappeared in a whirlwind of dark magic, leaving the four swan children alone on the lake.

For three hundred years, the Children of Lir lived on Lough Derravaragh. Though their bodies were changed, their hearts remained human, and they sang the most beautiful songs ever heard in Ireland. People would travel from far and wide to listen to the swans' music, not knowing they were hearing the voices of Lir's lost children.

The swan children sang of their homeland, of their father's palace beneath the waves, and of their hope that someday they would be free. Their music was so lovely that it could heal broken hearts and bring peace to troubled souls.

When the first three hundred years ended, the children flew to the stormy sea between Ireland and Scotland. Here the waters were rough and cold, and many nights they struggled against fierce winds and crashing waves. But still they sang, and sailors would hear their voices carrying across the water like a beacon of hope in the darkness.

Finally, after six hundred years as swans, they flew to the waters near Inishglora. By now, Christianity had come to Ireland, and the children could sometimes hear the faint sound of church bells ringing across the land. Their hearts filled with hope – perhaps their curse would soon be broken.

One morning, as the sun painted the sky in shades of gold and pink, the clear, sweet sound of church bells rang out across the water. Saint Patrick himself had come to the island and was celebrating mass.

As the bells rang, the four swans felt a familiar tingling in their feathers. The magic that had bound them for nine centuries was finally breaking. They swam quickly to shore, their hearts beating with excitement and hope.

But as they reached the beach, a terrible realization struck them. They were no longer swans, it was true — but they were no longer the young children they had been nine hundred years ago. The years had passed, and they had aged. They were now ancient, their hair white as their swan feathers had been, their bodies frail and bent.

Saint Patrick found them there on the shore and, understanding their story through divine insight, quickly baptized them and gave them his blessing. The Children of Lir had finally found peace.

As they lay dying, no longer bound by the curse, Fionnuala spoke for the last time with her beautiful voice: "We have suffered long, but we have also brought music to the world. Our song gave comfort to the lonely, hope to the despairing, and beauty to all who heard it. Perhaps that was the true purpose of our long journey."

The four children died peacefully, and it's said that their spirits flew together to join their father Lir in his palace beneath the waves. But their gift to the world lived on — for the most beautiful music in Ireland still echoes with the memory of the swans' song, and when people hear particularly lovely music across the water, they say, "Listen — the Children of Lir are singing."

Saint Patrick built a church on the spot where they had died, and travelers say that on quiet mornings, when the mist rises from the lake, you can still hear the faint sound of four voices singing together in perfect harmony — a reminder that even the cruelest magic cannot destroy the power of love, hope, and the beauty that comes from hearts that remain pure despite suffering.

Myths and Legends Word Search

```
D T A D J L A F F U R E G I X
R P X Y V X S A Z A I T J O A
U I W K M A G I C K I Y S C D
I Q A U W W T S L E R R B H G
D L B L D S A E D E C N Y A A
K T N A I G S R B W R F M N D
P W V M N E O M R M A I I G O
V A R O F S A I S I I N D E S
N M H I C H H E H M O N R L S
E Z O S C Z C E R Z R R O I Z
G A G P K P E P E K I C W N P
O X F I O N N K K O O H S G A
N F G R C U E N C H A N T E D
A B K A X M D D Y Y W Z O N V
N T K L Z A G F Y X L A H D O
R N U A H C E R P E L I D U A
I A K P V E M H A B G I R L Q
T D N E G E L K O Z W U E K Y
```

Aoife
Banshee
Chamber
Changeling
Dagda
Druid
Enchanted

Fairy
Finn
Fionn
Giant
Legend
Leprechaun
Lir

Magic
Mist
Selkie
Spiral
Sword
Tirnanog
Warrior

Celtic Tree of Life

To the ancient Celts, trees were magical. They believed every tree had a spirit and that forests were places of wisdom and connection. The Tree of Life shows a tree with branches reaching to the sky and roots digging deep into the earth — a symbol of balance, harmony, and the link between heaven and earth.

The Celts believed trees connected all living things, and that each tree held secrets of the universe. Cutting down a sacred tree was a serious offense! The Tree of Life also stood for strength, rebirth, and family — its endless knot of roots and branches showing how everything is connected.

Popular Sports

Ireland has a long history of exciting, fast-paced sports—from ancient field games to modern international competitions. Here are some favorites across the country.

Hurling

Hurling is one of the fastest field sports in the world—and one of the oldest! It's been played in Ireland for more than 3,000 years. Players use a flat wooden stick called a hurley to hit a small leather ball called a sliotar. The goal is to score by sending the sliotar into the opposing team's net or over the goalposts.

Hurling is fast, exciting, and full of skill. Players must run, catch, hit, and even balance the ball on their hurley while dodging defenders. It's like a mix of hockey, baseball, and lacrosse—all with an Irish twist!

Gaelic Football

Gaelic football is Ireland's most-played sport, and it's completely unique. It looks a bit like soccer, but also a little like basketball and rugby! Players use a round ball slightly smaller than a soccer ball. They can kick it, carry it, bounce it, or pass it with their hands—just not throw it.

Each team tries to score by either kicking the ball into the goal (worth 3 points) or over the crossbar between two tall posts (worth 1 point). The game is fast, physical, and full of action from start to finish. It's played on a large field with 15 players per team, and the biggest matches happen at Croke Park, Ireland's famous stadium in Dublin.

⚽ Soccer (Football)

Soccer—called "football" in Ireland and most of the world—is also a favorite sport. Kids play it at school, in backyards, and with local clubs. Ireland has its own national teams for men and women, and big games often bring the whole country together.

Many Irish players go on to play for teams across Europe. While Gaelic football and hurling are more traditional, soccer is the international sport most young Irish players grow up watching on TV and playing with their friends. Some towns even fly team flags on match days!

🏉 Rugby

Rugby is a tough, team-based sport played with an oval ball. It's full of tackles, passes, and powerful scrums where teams push against each other for control. In Ireland, rugby is extra special because players from both the Republic of Ireland and Northern Ireland play on the same national team—one of the only sports where the island competes as one.

What is the GAA?

The Gaelic Athletic Association (GAA) was founded in 1884 to protect Irish games like hurling and Gaelic football. Today, it runs thousands of local clubs and holds huge events like the All-Ireland Final at Croke Park in Dublin.

Ireland's rugby team is one of the best in the world and regularly plays in the Six Nations Championship against countries like England, France, and Italy. Whether you're watching a local club match or an international test game, rugby is full of drama and teamwork.

 Horse Racing

Horse racing has a long history in Ireland and is one of the country's most popular spectator sports. Ireland's green countryside and mild climate make it a perfect place to raise and train horses. Some of the world's most famous racehorses come from Irish farms.

There are races held all over Ireland throughout the year—from small-town tracks to major events like the Irish Grand National. Many families attend races as a fun day out, and some people travel from all over the world to watch or bet on their favorite horses. Irish jockeys, trainers, and horses are famous in places as far away as the UK, America, and Australia.

Did You Know?

- The All-Ireland Final draws over 80,000 fans to Croke Park.
- Hurling may date back over 3,000 years!
- Horse racing is one of Ireland's oldest spectator sports.

Mini-Quiz
1. In Gaelic football, what are two ways to score points?
2. Which stadium in Dublin holds over 80,000 fans?
3. What two parts of Ireland join together to play on the same rugby team?
4. What sport involves jockeys and racing animals with hooves?
5. What does the GAA stand for?

Maze Game

Help the football (soccer) player score a goal.

The Salmon of Knowledge

Young Fionn MacCumhaill had always been curious about everything. While other boys played with wooden swords, Fionn asked endless questions about the world around him.

When Fionn turned fifteen, his mother sent him to learn from Finnegas, the wisest poet in Ireland. Fionn found the old man sitting beside a deep pool on the River Boyne, staring intently at the dark water.

"I am Fionn MacCumhaill," the boy said politely. "I've come to learn from you."

Finnegas looked up, his eyes twinkling with ancient wisdom. "Welcome, young Fionn. Let me tell you why I sit here day after day."

The old poet pointed to the water. "In these depths swims the Salmon of Knowledge, the wisest creature in the world. This salmon ate nine hazelnuts of wisdom that fell from a sacred tree. Whoever catches and eats this fish will gain all knowledge. I have waited seven years, for prophecy says someone named Fionn will receive the salmon's wisdom."

Every day, Fionn helped Finnegas fish while learning about poetry, history, and Ireland's old stories. "True wisdom," Finnegas taught, "comes from understanding how all things are connected."

One misty morning, the line finally grew taut. "This is it!" Finnegas cried. After a fierce struggle, he landed the most beautiful fish Fionn had ever seen. Its scales shimmered with rainbow colors, and its eyes held ancient knowledge.

"Quick, gather wood for a fire," Finnegas commanded. "We must cook this immediately. But listen carefully — you must not eat even the smallest bit. The first person to taste it gains all its knowledge, and after seven years of waiting, that must be me."

Fionn tended the fire carefully as the magical salmon cooked. The smell was incredible — not just fish, but wisdom itself. As it cooked, a blister formed on the salmon's skin. Without thinking, Fionn pressed it down to help it cook evenly.

The hot blister burst, splashing burning oil onto Fionn's thumb. "Ow!" he cried, instinctively putting his thumb in his mouth.

The moment his thumb touched his tongue, the world exploded with knowledge. Suddenly Fionn understood the language of birds, the whispers of wind, and secrets of the deep ocean.

He knew the history of every tree and the name of every star.

When Finnegas saw the wonder in Fionn's eyes, he smiled with joy instead of disappointment. "The prophecy is fulfilled. You are the Fionn meant to receive the salmon's wisdom. I was destined to catch it, but you were meant to gain its knowledge."

"What should I do with this gift?" Fionn asked.

"Use it to protect Ireland and help her people," Finnegas replied. "Knowledge without kindness is useless."

From that day forward, whenever Fionn needed wisdom, he would put his thumb to his mouth and the knowledge would come. He became Ireland's greatest hero, leading the Fianna warriors not just with strength, but with wisdom.

Years later, Fionn often visited his old teacher by the river. "Do you regret not eating the salmon yourself?" he once asked.

Finnegas shook his head, eyes twinkling. "The greatest knowledge I gained was learning that sometimes a teacher's most important job is helping someone else reach their destiny. Watching you become the hero Ireland needed has been worth more than all the wisdom in the world."

And so the legend reminds us that true wisdom lies not just in what we know, but in how we use our knowledge to make the world better.

Word Scramble
Unscramble the words using the clues.

1. CASLET   _ _ _ _ _ _
Ireland has hundreds of these ancient buildings.

2. RAPDAE   _ _ _ _ _ _
A fun part of St. Patrick's Day.

3. YRFAI   _ _ _ _ _
Tiny magical beings in Irish folklore.

4. IKTCRAP   _ _ _ _ _ _ _
The saint who drove out the snakes.

5. ECOTGTA   _ _ _ _ _ _ _
A cozy home in the Irish countryside.

6. REAEVNRIDC   _ _ _ _ _ _ _ _ _ _
A world-famous Irish dance show.

7. OSATOPET   _ _ _ _ _ _ _ _
A key part of Irish history and food.

8. IVTLSEFA   _ _ _ _ _ _ _ _
Where you'll find music, food, and fun!

9. ERENG   _ _ _ _ _
The color most associated with Ireland.

10. IDTATRNIO   _ _ _ _ _ _ _ _ _
Something passed down through generations.

Myths and Legends Crossword

Use what you've learned in this book to solve the puzzle.

Across

3 Tiny supernatural beings from Irish tales (5)
4 Another word for a traditional story (4)
8 Magical fish that holds the wisdom of the world (6)
9 Old poet who taught Fionn by the river (8)
11 Sea god and father of four children (3)
13 Magical bird shape the Children of Lir became (4)
14 A whispered magical phrase (5)
15 Someone admired for bravery or good deeds (4)
18 Another word for loud crying (4)
19 What makes fairy tales and legends so powerful (5)
20 Sound the banshee makes (7)
21 A very old story told again and again (6)

Down

1 Ghostly woman who cries when someone is about to die (7)
2 Hero who accidentally gained great wisdom (5)
4 Irish holiday with costumes and bonfires (6)
5 Nut that gave the salmon its wisdom (8)
6 Stepmother who cursed the children of Lir (5)
7 Summer tradition with big flames and community fun (7)
10 Ireland's patron saint (2,7)
12 Ancient Irish holiday with costumes and bonfires (7)
16 A powerful magical punishment (5)
17 Body of water where Lir's children were trapped (4)

Wild Ireland

From misty mountains to rocky cliffs and rolling green fields, Ireland's landscape is full of dramatic beauty. You'll find quiet forests, wide-open boglands, and crashing waves along its wild Atlantic coast.

And where there's wild land, there's wild life! Ireland is home to a mix of native and introduced animals — from mountain-climbing goats to puffins perched on sea cliffs. Some animals are shy and rare, while others might peek at you from a grassy field or bark from a wave.

Irish Hare

Fast, fluffy, and full of energy! This unique hare lives only in Ireland and can race up to 40 mph across open fields.

Puffin

Wearing a "clown beak" and waddling like a penguin, the puffin is one of Ireland's silliest seabirds. Look for them on cliff edges in the summer!

Irish Wolfhound

Tall as a small pony and as gentle as a lamb! These giant dogs were once fierce wolf hunters — now they're just lovable, long-legged friends.

Grey Seal

These whiskered swimmers love to nap on rocks or peek up from the waves. You might hear them barking on the beach!

Pine Marten

This tree-climbing, squirrel-chasing mammal is super sneaky! Once nearly extinct, it's now bouncing back in Irish woodlands.

Feral Goats

These scruffy explorers live wild in rocky hills and mountains. No one owns them — they climb where they please!

Barn Owl

This ghostly bird glides silently at night, hunting mice in the moonlight. You'll spot its heart-shaped face if you're very quiet!

Brilliant Irish Inventions

Ireland has a long history of clever ideas and world-changing inventions! From machines that fly underwater to early computers, these inventors helped shape the modern world.

Invention Matching Game

Match the inventions with the person who invented them.

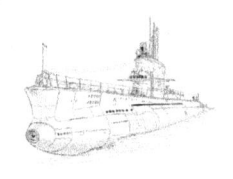 **Submarine**	**Harry Ferguson** — Made farming easier for farmers everywhere
 **Color Photography**	**Sir James Martin** — Helped pilots blast out of airplanes safely
 **Tractor**	**John Philip Holland** — Loved the sea and designed something that dives beneath it
 **Airplane Ejector Seat**	**Kay McNulty** — Born in Donegal, she was a math whiz who worked on early machines
 **Induction Coil**	**John Joly** — Irish scientist who used light and color to solve problems
 **Computer Programming**	**Nicholas Callan** — A priest who worked with magnets and electricity

Daily Irish Life Word Search

```
Y I I P U Z T Z U L K Y I R S
E F A R M E R S U R Q M D J A
X W P N R Q R M R U D M Q H D
H T X N R W S B S N J A Z K T
S O I J Y E D P L N W M X X W
C E J F I M S O Z E Z A E O E
B R D L A I O Z L R N R W L T
K I L F R W X E S J C Y D S
L E S C R B L P B R U H Y M T
W S B C E Y A H U X M I E C O
T E A C U K Y R Z B P P L O B
S D C A P I T G M N E S L E C
X Q S N U Y T I L B R E O D I
T R A C T O R Y E I R H R A Q
Y F D A R B A D O S Y A T M U
W X S P Z N L H H D Z A C A R
C I A R C O T N I C Z C D K N
N I B C L K F S O O T Y A T L
```

Barmbrack	Farmers	Stew
Bin	Fry	Tayto
Biscuit	Jumper	Tea
Cap	Mammy	Tractor
Chips	Pub	Trolley
Craic	Runners	Wellies
Crisps	Soda Brad	Wool

The Banshee: Ireland's Mysterious Spirit

In Irish folklore, the Banshee is a ghostly woman who appears when someone is about to die. But don't worry—she doesn't cause death. She's more like a warning signal, letting a family know that a loved one is passing away.

The word "banshee" comes from the Irish words "bean sídhe", which means "woman of the fairy mound." She's considered a type of fairy spirit, not a witch or a monster.

👻 What Does a Banshee Look Like?

Banshees are said to have long hair and wear flowing clothes, often white or gray, though some legends describe her with red or silver eyes from crying so much. She may appear as a young woman, a middle-aged washerwoman, or an old crone.

☠ What Does She Do?

Most famously, the Banshee wails or cries when someone is about to die. Her voice is said to be high and piercing—so sad it can chill your bones. People say if you hear the Banshee's cry near your home, it means someone in your family may soon pass away.

But in some stories, she just sits quietly, brushing her hair near a stream or walking silently at night.

Did You Know?

In some tales, the Banshee is seen washing bloodstained clothes at a river, which is why she's sometimes called the "Washer at the Ford."

Not all Banshees are terrifying! In older legends, she was simply a family spirit who cared deeply for the people she watched over.

It's said that Banshees only appear to old Irish families with names starting with O' or Mac, like O'Connor or MacMahon.

Real or Legend?

Many people have claimed to hear the cry of a Banshee—but no one has ever captured one on camera or told the same story twice. Whether she's a real spirit or just a way to explain the sadness of loss, the Banshee remains one of the most famous and mysterious figures in Irish folklore.

Word Scramble
Unscramble the words using the clues.

1. **FSCFLI** _ _ _ _ _ _
   Ireland has some dramatic ones by the sea!

2. **ERNIALD** _ _ _ _ _ _ _
   The Emerald Isle!

3. **CILTEC** _ _ _ _ _ _
   Ancient Irish culture and symbols.

4. **PRHA** _ _ _ _
   TIreland's national musical instrument.

5. **BNRLAEY** _ _ _ _ _ _ _
   A famous stone you kiss for luck.

6. **PREHEANLCU** _ _ _ _ _ _ _ _ _ _
   A mischievous little fairy with gold.

7. **IDLUNB** _ _ _ _ _ _
   Ireland's capital city.

8. **ROKAHSCM** _ _ _ _ _ _ _ _
   A three-leaf plant and Irish symbol.

9. **WNBRIOA** _ _ _ _ _ _ _
   Said to lead to a pot of gold!

10. **LICGEA** _ _ _ _ _ _
    A traditional Irish language.

Irish Slang Crossword

Use what you've learned in this book to solve the puzzle.

Across

3 Funny or hilarious (3)
5 Truck (5)
7 Sweater (6)
8 A fun time with friends or laughter (5)
10 Friends (5)
11 Chips (6)
14 Flashlight (5)
16 Where you toss your trash (3)
17 Expensive (4)
20 Fine/okay (5)
21 Stroller (4)
22 Shopping cart (7)
23 Another word for really nice (6)

Down

1 Slang for mouth (3)
2 Tired (7)
4 Candy (6)
6 Trash (7)
9 Police (5)
12 Favorite place for adults to meet and chat (3)
13 Vacation (7)
15 French fries (5)
18 Silly person or fool (5)
19 Yard (6)

Ancient Celtic Symbols

Long ago, the Celts used special symbols to represent ideas like love, strength, life, and nature. These designs often had no beginning or end — just like the cycle of seasons, the bonds of family, and the mysteries of life.

Here are some of the most famous Celtic symbols still seen in Ireland today:

Triskelion (Triple Spiral)

Three swirling arms joined at the center. This ancient symbol may stand for life, death, and rebirth — or land, sea, and sky. You'll find it carved into ancient stones like at Newgrange.

Celtic Knot

A looped design with no beginning or end. Often used to show never-ending friendship, love, or faith. These knots decorate jewelry, stone carvings, and old books.

Claddagh Ring

A heart held by two hands with a crown on top. This symbol means love (heart), friendship (hands), and loyalty (crown). It's a famous Irish gift.

Draw Your Own Celtic Symbol:

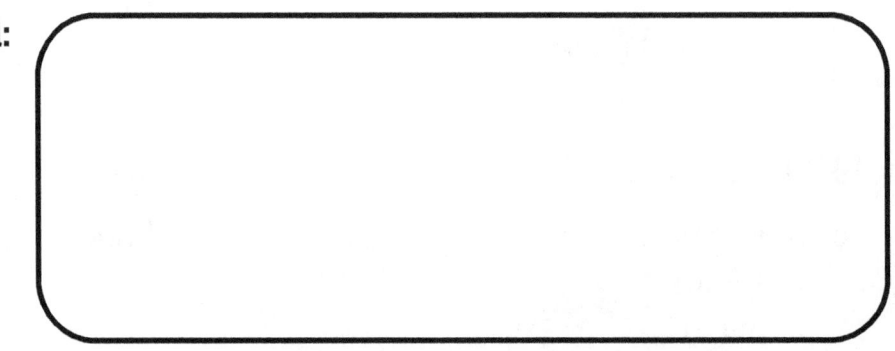

Taste of Ireland

Ireland has a rich food culture full of cozy, hearty dishes. Many traditional meals come from simple farm ingredients like potatoes, root vegetables, and meat. Here are some favorites still eaten today!

Irish Stew
Made with lamb or beef, potatoes, carrots, and onions — warm and filling on cold days!

Boxty
A potato pancake often served with butter or bacon. Crisp on the outside, soft inside!

Soda Bread
A round loaf made without yeast. Best with jam and butter!

What Would You Eat?
Design your own Irish meal! Draw it on the plate below.

Sounds of Ireland

Irish music is famous around the world! It's full of fast rhythms, lively melodies, and toe-tapping beats. Traditional Irish music is often played with special instruments. Let's learn about a few!

Bodhrán (say it: bow-rawn)

The bodhrán is a round Irish drum played with a short stick called a tipper. Musicians hold it under one arm and tap different rhythms with the other. It's often called the heartbeat of Irish music — you can feel the beat in your chest!

Fiddle

The fiddle looks just like a violin, but in Ireland, it's played with a different style — fast, bouncy, and full of energy! Fiddlers can make people want to dance in seconds. Some even learn to play by ear instead of reading music.

Tin Whistle

Also known as a penny whistle, this little flute is easy to carry and fun to play. It has six holes and makes a bright, cheerful sound. Many Irish kids learn it as their first instrument — maybe you could too!

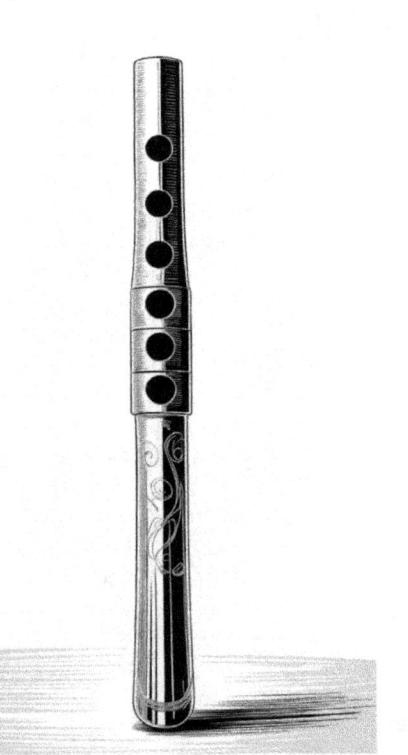

Design Your Own Musical Instrument

Draw your own traditional Irish instrument. What does it sound like? What's it made of?

Who? What? Where? Crossword

Use what you've learned in this book to solve the puzzle.

Across

3 Irish dish with meat and potatoes (4)

5 Musical instrument and national symbol (4)

8 A person who writes poems (4)

9 Big fluffy Irish dog breed (5)

11 Ancient stone site older than the pyramids (9)

13 Ancient book filled with glowing artwork (4,2,5)

15 Singer known for haunting songs and long red hair (4)

16 An Irish instrument often played in pubs (6)

17 Kiss the Blarney _____ (5)

Down

1 Author of Dracula (6)

2 A terrible time when crops fail (6)

4 Drum used in Irish music (7)

6 Colors of Irish flag are white, green, and _____ (6)

7 First woman president of Ireland (8)

8 Ireland's most famous saint (7)

10 Another word for Irish language (6)

12 Irish poet who won Nobel Prize (5)

13 Scientist known as father of chemistry (5)

14 Irish word for Ireland (4)

Word Scramble
Unscramble the words using the clues.

1. EHSEP — _ _ _ _ _
These animals graze all over Irish hills!

2. VROCEL — _ _ _ _ _ _
A lucky plant often found in Irish fields.

3. HTMY — _ _ _ _
A story told long ago, often magical.

4. SHROE IRNGAC — _ _ _ _ _ _ _ _ _ _ _
A fast-paced sport popular at Irish tracks.

5. EACND — _ _ _ _ _
Ireland is famous for this fast-stepping art.

6. RRKEY — _ _ _ _ _
A beautiful county in the southwest of Ireland.

7. YEORLTSRLTE — _ _ _ _ _ _ _ _ _ _ _
Someone who shares Irish myths and legends.

8. SWSAN — _ _ _ _ _
Magical creatures in Irish legends.

9. SOSENT — _ _ _ _ _ _
Ireland's ancient ruins are full of these.

10. CRLKEIMI — _ _ _ _ _ _ _ _
A funny five-line Irish poem.

Label the Map

Label the cities and bodies of water in the map below.

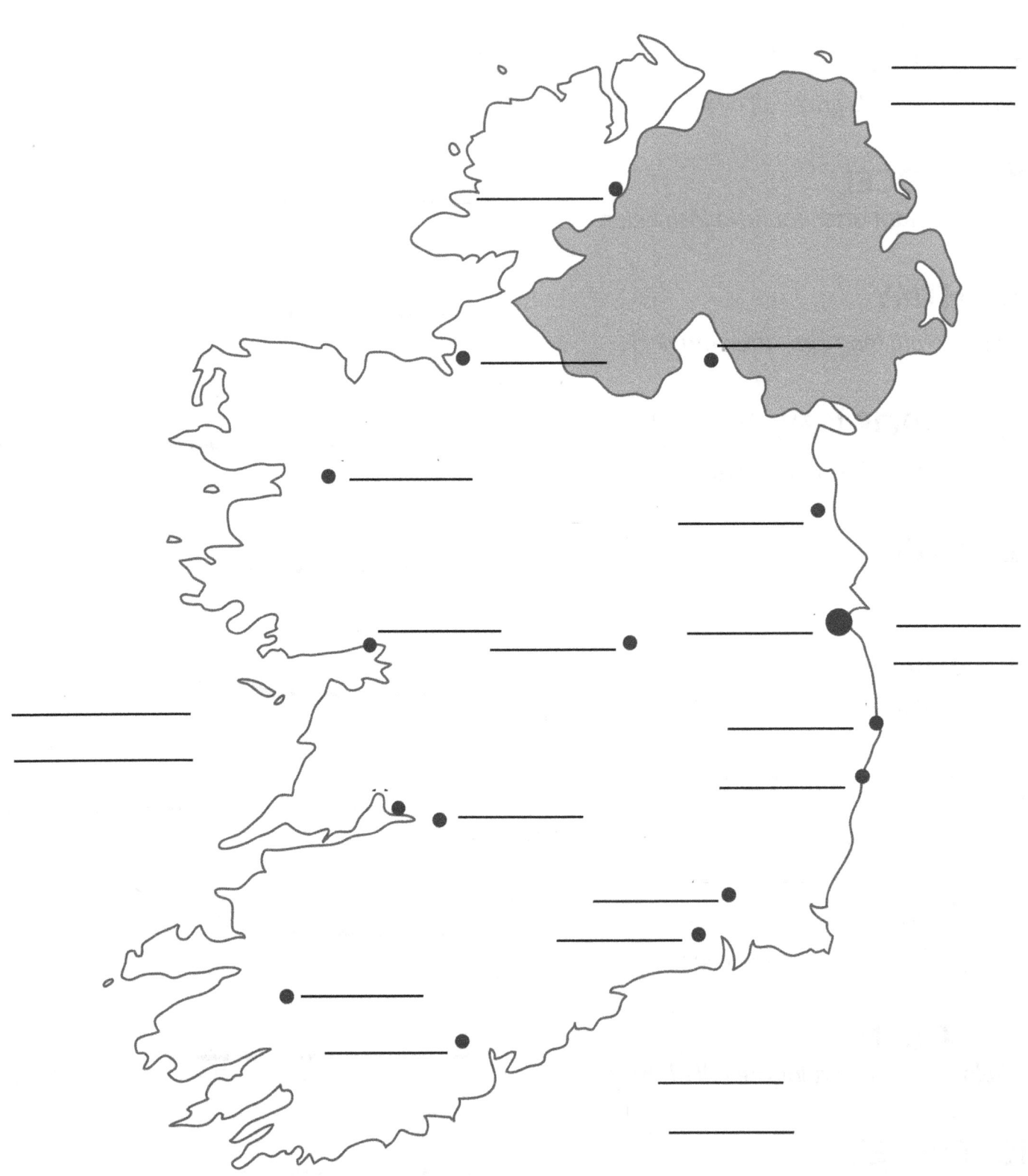

Ireland Quiz

Test your knowledge about Ireland. Circle the correct answer.

1 What is the capital of Ireland?

   a) Belfast
   b) Dublin
   c) Cork
   d) Galway

2 What colors are on the Irish flag?

   a) Green, white, and orange
   b) Blue, green, and white
   c) Red, white, green
   d) Green, gold, silver

3 Which animal is a famous Irish dog breed?

   a) Golden retriever
   b) Irish Wolfhound
   c) Border collie
   d) Corgi

4 What ancient book is filled with colorful Celtic art?

   a) Book of Lir
   b) The Green Book
   c) Book of Kells
   d) The Fairy Chronicles

5 What kind of animal were the Children of Lir turned into?

   a) Owls
   b) Seals
   c) Swans
   d) Wolves

6 What is Gaelic football most like?

   a) Baseball
   b) Basketball
   c) A mix of soccer and rugby
   d) Ice hockey

7 Which of these is a traditional Irish holiday?

   a) Thanksgiving
   b) Bonfire Night
   c) Fourth of July
   d) Mardi Gras

8 How many provinces does Ireland have?

   a) Two
   b) Four
   c) Six
   d) Ten

9 What is Ireland's national symbol?

   a) Clover
   b) Harp
   c) Celtic Knot
   d) Eagle

10 Which of these is a Celtic symbol that represents balance?

   a) Triskelion
   b) Tree of Life
   c) Stone circle
   d) Rock knot

Answers

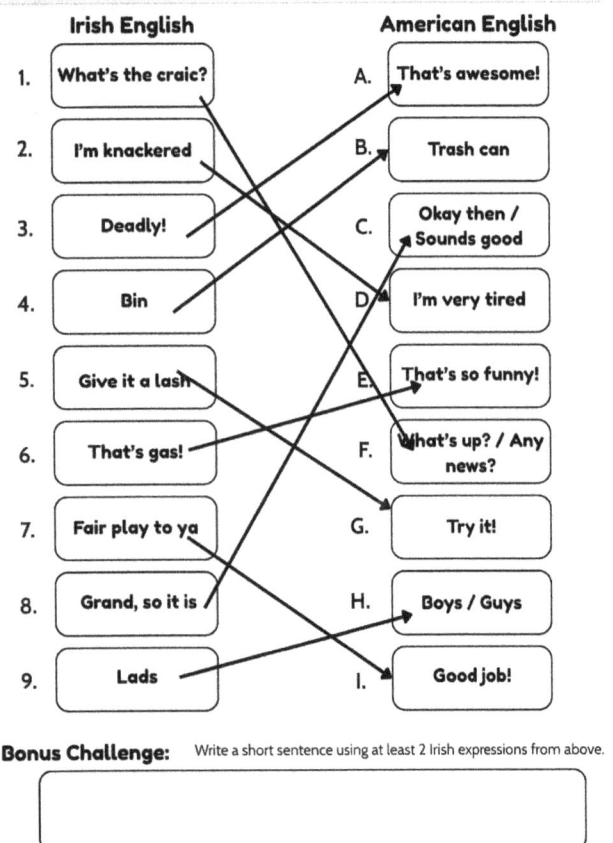

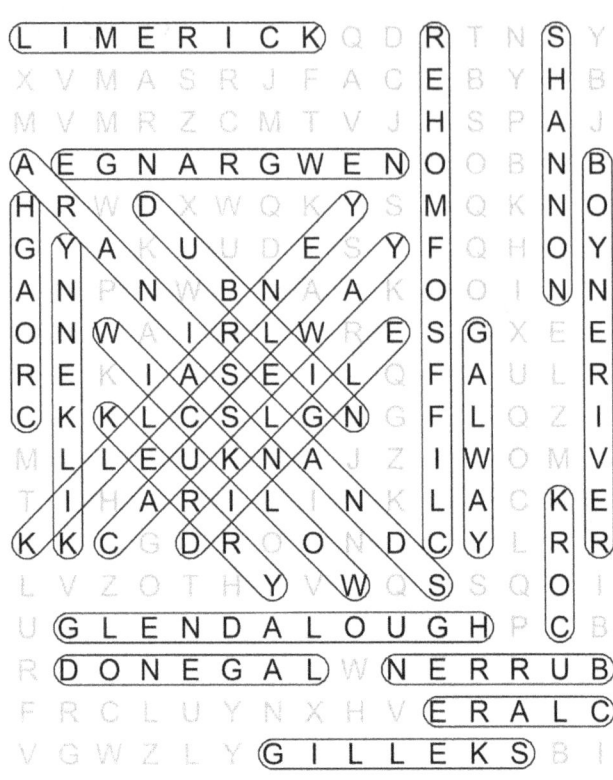

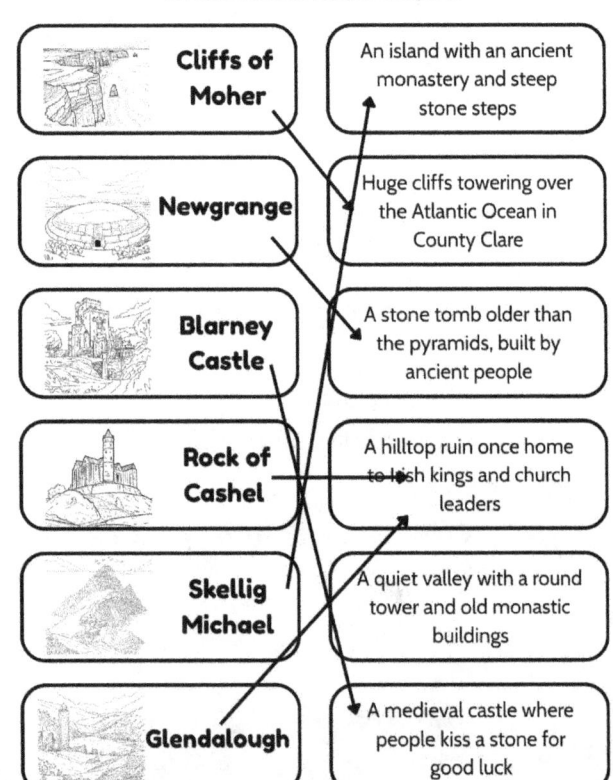

Answers

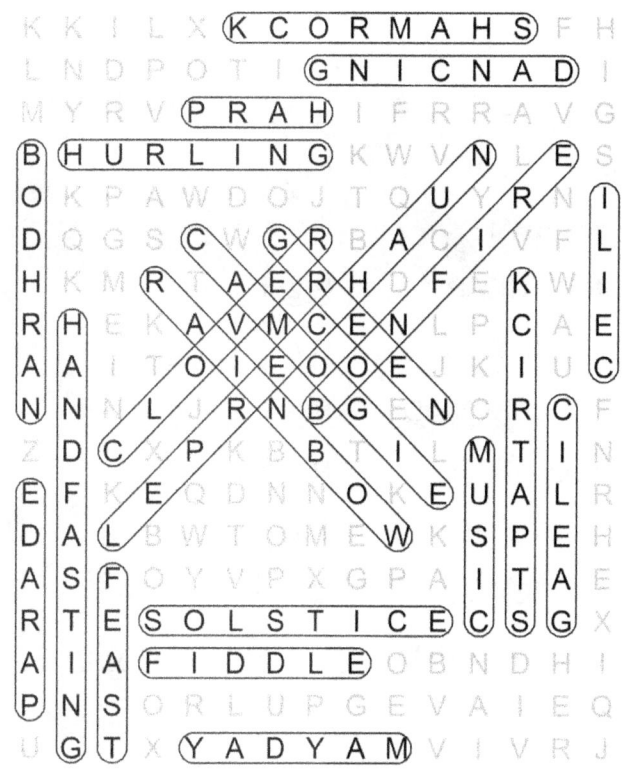
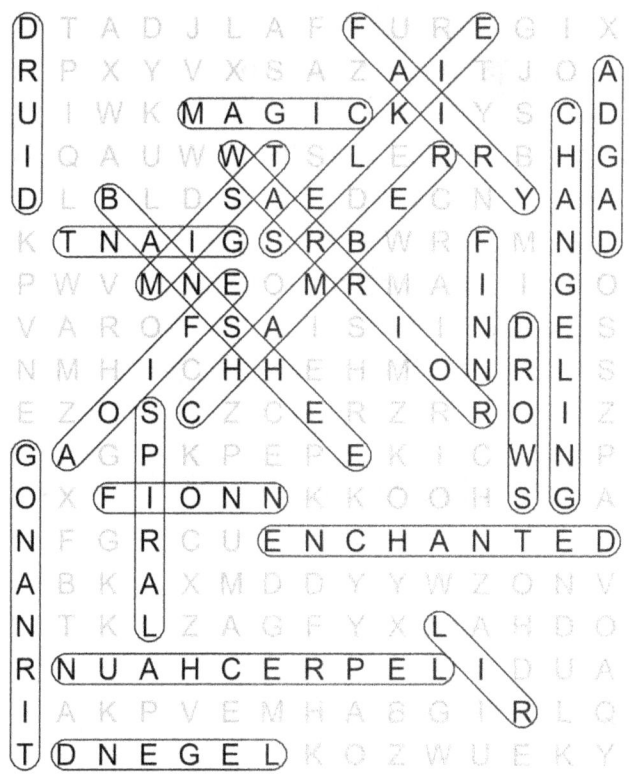

Answers

1. CASLET — <u>Castle</u>
2. RAPDAE — <u>Parade</u>
3. YRFAI — <u>Fairy</u>
4. IKTCRAP — <u>Patrick</u>
5. ECOTGTA — <u>Cottage</u>
6. REAEVNRIDC — <u>Riverdance</u>
7. OSATOPET — <u>Potatoes</u>
8. IVTLSEFA — <u>Festival</u>
9. ERENG — <u>Green</u>
10. IDTATRNIO — <u>Tradition</u>

Invention Matching Game

Match the inventions with the person who invented them.

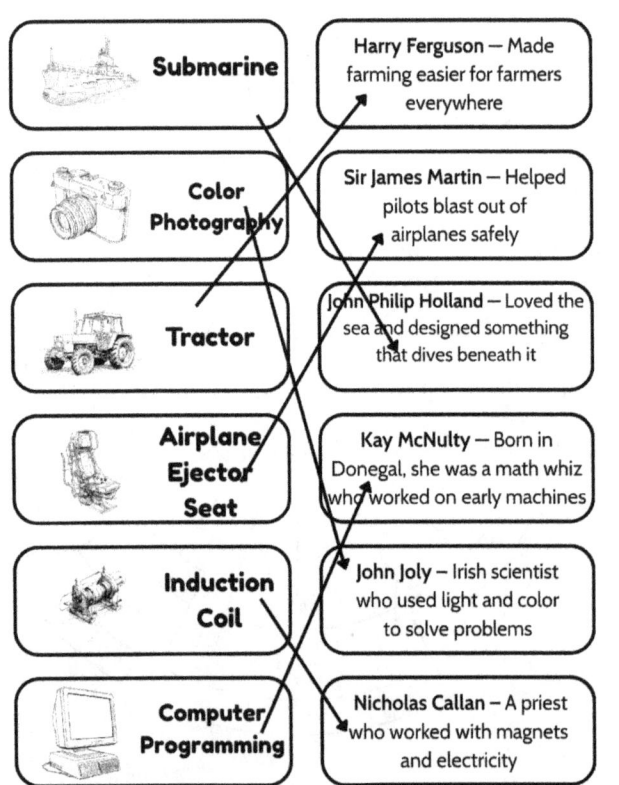

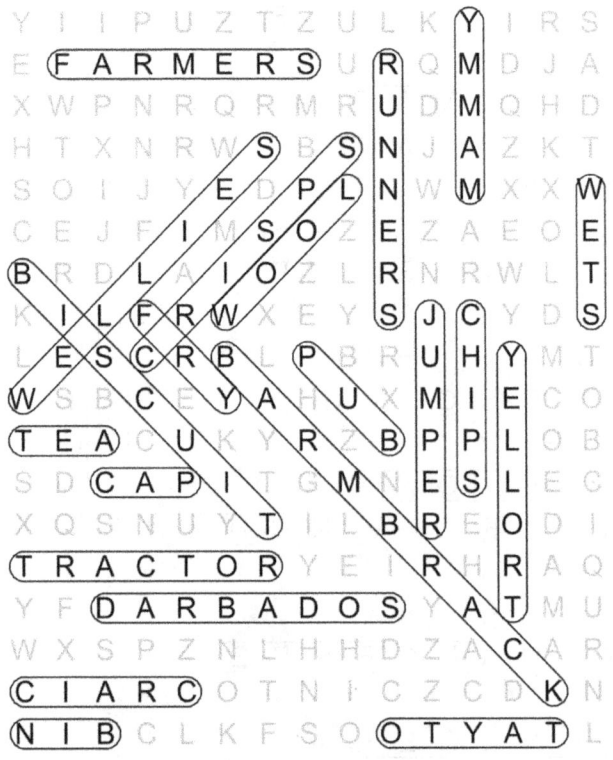

Answers

1. FSCFLI — Cliffs
2. ERNIALD — Ireland
3. CILTEC — Celtic
4. PRHA — Harp
5. BNRLAEY — Blarney
6. PREHEANLCU — Leprechaun
7. IDLUNB — Dublin
8. ROKAHSCM — Shamrock
9. WNBRIOA — Rainbow
10. LICGEA — Gaelic

1. EHSEP — Sheep
2. VROCEL — Clover
3. HTMY — Myth
4. SHROE IRNGAC — Horse racing
5. EACND — Dance
6. RRKEY — Kerry
7. YEORLTSRLTE — Storyteller
8. SSWAN — Swans
9. SOSENT — Stones
10. CRLKEIMI — Limerick

Answers

Ireland Quiz

Test your knowledge about Ireland. Circle the correct answer.

1 What is the capital of Ireland?
a) Belfast
(b) Dublin
c) Cork
d) Galway

2 What colors are on the Irish flag?
a) Green, white, and orange
b) Blue, green, and white
c) Red, white, green
d) Green, gold, silver

3 Which animal is a famous Irish dog breed?
a) Golden retriever
b) Irish Wolfhound
c) Border collie
d) Corgi

4 What ancient book is filled with colorful Celtic art?
a) Book of Lir
b) The Green Book
c) Book of Kells
d) The Fairy Chronicles

5 What kind of animal were the Children of Lir turned into?
a) Owls
b) Seals
c) Swans
d) Wolves

6 What is Gaelic football most like?
a) Baseball
b) Basketball
c) A mix of soccer and rugby
d) Ice hockey

7 Which of these is a traditional Irish holiday?
a) Thanksgiving
b) Bonfire Night
c) Fourth of July
d) Mardi Gras

8 How many provinces does Ireland have?
a) Two
b) Four
c) Six
d) Ten

9 What is Ireland's national symbol?
a) Clover
b) Harp
c) Celtic Knot
d) Eagle

10 Which of these is a Celtic symbol that represents balance?
a) Triskelion
b) Tree of Life
c) Stone circle
d) Rock knot